I0013078

Department of Homeland Security

CYBER STORM III
Final Report

July 2011

**Department of Homeland Security
Office of Cybersecurity and Communications
National Cyber Security Division**

CYBER STORM III
FINAL REPORT
TABLE OF CONTENTS

EXECUTIVE SUMMARY

The National Cyber Exercise: Cyber Storm (CS) is the Department of Homeland Security's (DHS) capstone national-level cybersecurity exercise and represents the Nation's most extensive cybersecurity exercise effort of its kind. Cyber Storm is a Homeland Security Exercise and Evaluation Program (HSEEP) Tier II exercise focusing on federal strategy and policy. The Department's National Cyber Security Division (NCSD) sponsors the exercise to improve the capabilities of the cyber incident response community; encouraging the advancement of public–private partnerships within the critical infrastructure sectors and strengthening relationships between the Federal Government and partners at the state, local, and international levels. CS III included participation from 8 Cabinet-level departments, 13 states, 12 international partners, and approximately 60 private-sector companies and coordination bodies. Participation focused on the information technology (IT), communications, energy (electric), chemical, and transportation critical infrastructure sectors and incorporated various levels of play from other critical infrastructure sectors. Together, these entities participated in the design, execution, and post-exercise analysis of the largest, most comprehensive Government-led, full-scale cyber exercise to date. Participants exercised their ability to prepare for, protect from, and respond to cyber attacks and execute current national cybersecurity plans and capabilities. Players responded to simulated attacks according to established policies and procedures. No actual networks were targeted or affected during the exercise. Participants successfully executed CS III between September 27 and October 1, 2010, at player locations across the United States and internationally, with the main Exercise Control (ExCon) cell located at U.S. Secret Service (USSS) Headquarters in Washington, D.C.

KEY ACHIEVEMENTS

CS III served as a catalyst for significant learning and operational analysis for the cyber incident response community. Throughout CS III, the participant set—

- Demonstrated the efficacy of the National Cyber Incident Response Plan (NCIRP) and identified areas requiring refinement;
- Navigated a response to a Significant Cyber Incident with support from the interagency, states, private-sector, and international organizations;
- Assessed the operation of the National Cybersecurity and Communications Integration Center (NCCIC) during a Significant Cyber Incident and identified areas for improved coordination and communication within the NCCIC and with its partners;
- Incorporated significant senior leadership participation across the public and private sectors, which helped during key decision points;
- Demonstrated the benefits of organized, efficient, cohesive, and action oriented interagency and public-private coordination and decision-making;
- Integrated private-sector participants into operations, information sharing, and action planning and identified areas of focus necessary to effectively respond to a Significant Cyber Incident;
- Reinforced existing coordination mechanisms and continued to facilitate new relationships within the cyber incident response community throughout the exercise planning process; and,

- Identified and catalogued needs related to situational awareness, information sharing, and consistent messaging across the cyber incident response community.

EXERCISE PLANNING STRUCTURE

The Exercise Planning Team divided the 18-month planning process into five distinct stages that support planning, execution, and evaluation of the CS III exercise. Within each stage, a series of events, milestones, and general planning goals moved the process forward. Throughout the process, significant cross-community interaction, public–private collaboration, and information sharing supported increased awareness of cyber-based threats, their potential implications, and the current response framework.

SCENARIO

To create the CS III scenario, NCSD organized a Scenario Team, leveraging the engagement and technical expertise of private sector operators, that developed initial core scenario conditions and advised further scenario customization efforts throughout the planning process. The Scenario Team contributed to coordinated scenario development, creating a forum to vet, discuss, and achieve consensus on core scenario conditions that could be applied to participating organizations. The use of core scenario conditions as the basis for all targeted attacks ensured the exercise represented a comprehensive national and internationally Significant Cyber Incident. In developing these specifics, team members incorporated CS III goals and objectives, previous exercise findings, and previous lessons learned into scenario design—while adhering to the exercise construct.

During CS III, players responded to a series of simulated, targeted attacks resulting from compromises to the Domain Name System (DNS) and the Internet chain of trust (i.e., validity of certificates and Certificate Authorities [CAs]). Because of the reliance on DNS and the chain of trust for a wide range of Internet functions, transactions, and communications, the adversary challenged players' ability to operate in a trusted environment, complete trusted transactions, and support critical functions. In addition, the adversary used these compromises to carry out a variety of targeted attacks against private-sector companies, select critical infrastructure sectors, public-sector enterprises, and international counterparts. The scenario construct ensured all exercise players felt the effects the core scenario created. Overall response required significant communication and coordination among a distributed and diverse player set, including private-sector, IT/Communications (IT/Comms) partners, and state and federal entities.

PUBLIC AFFAIRS AND VERY IMPORTANT PERSON VISITOR PROGRAM

Public Affairs

The Exercise Planning Team, in close coordination with the DHS Office of Public Affairs (OPA), the Office of Cybersecurity and Communications (CS&C) External Affairs Program, and NCSD's Outreach and Awareness Program, developed and implemented a robust Public Affairs (PA) Program to position CS III as a critical component of the Nation's efforts to promote an assured and resilient cyber infrastructure. The program incorporated input from real-world PA representatives from participating organizations.

Very Important Person Visitor Program

DHS created and conducted the Very Important Person (VIP) Visitor Program for CS III to highlight the importance of stakeholder partnerships across the cyber incident response community. The program provided senior-level invitees with an overview of the CS Exercise

Series and the opportunity to observe CS III execution from ExCon. Participants gained an in-depth understanding of their organization's involvement in the exercise and the subsequent impact of their organization's participation through these activities.

KEY FINDINGS

Information gathered throughout exercise planning and execution, post-exercise activities, and through the submission of post-exercise questionnaires revealed five significant high-level findings. These findings, outlined below, incorporate perspectives of CS III participants representing the Federal Government, state and local government, coordination bodies, the private sector, and international partners. They affect the cybersecurity community at large.

Finding 1
The NCIRP provides a sound framework for steady-state activities[1] and cyber incident response; however, the supporting processes, procedures, roles, and responsibilities outlined in the Plan require maturity. To truly serve as the framework for national-level cyber incident response, NCIRP concepts need to be further integrated into supporting Standard Operating Procedures (SOPs) and Concepts of Operations (CONOPS), complementary response plans, and corresponding partner operating procedures.

Finding 2
Cyber response collaboration among private-sector companies has advanced because of targeted initiatives and understanding of mutual benefit. Although public–private interaction around cyber response is continually evolving and improving, it can be complicated by the lack of timely and meaningful shared situational awareness; uncertainties regarding roles and responsibilities; and legal, customer, and/or security concerns.

Finding 3
To foster common awareness and support decision-making during a crisis, development, distribution, and maintenance of shared situational awareness—sometimes referred to as a common operating picture (COP) or, in this case, a cyber COP—across the community is a critical requirement. To be most effective, this shared situational awareness should be continuously maintained in steady state and incorporate resources and inputs from all stakeholders.

Finding 4
The National Cyber Risk Alert Level (NCRAL) is intended to inform preparedness, decision-making, information-sharing requirements, and cyber incident management activities. To increase NCRAL effectiveness, the thresholds that precipitate an alert level change, the communications and messaging that accompany a level change, and the recommended security posture and actions at each level must be further defined, widely distributed, and incorporated into organizational SOPs, Operations Plans, and CONOPS.

Finding 5
The Government, the private sector, and the general public rely on timely, accurate, and actionable public and strategic communication to manage threats to their networks and

---

[1] CS III execution primarily evaluated the transition from steady state to cyber incident response and cyber incident response actions outlined in the NCIRP. However, the ability to share the draft NCIRP with stakeholders across the public and private sectors allowed for several aspects of the steady state to be evaluated and assessed.

systems. The development and delivery of effective products and public statements are critical to coordinating an effective cyber response and maintaining public confidence during an incident.

CS III provided a realistic environment for organizations to assess their cyber response capabilities. DHS and participating organizations worked closely to establish the exercise's goals and to design a realistic scenario that met those goals and challenged players' response plans and activities. In addition, CS III allowed the community to coordinate a national-level response to a Significant Cyber Incident as outlined in the interim NCIRP.[2] CS III helped to position the NCIRP within the cyber incident response community and allowed the community to identify areas for refinement of the plan and corresponding procedures and operations. As part of exercise play, controllers identified significant findings and actions at the national, sector, and organizational level that the cyber incident response community will need to address. Through this interaction, participants forged and strengthened relationships across the cybersecurity community.

---

[2] Players exercised NCIRP, Interim Version, September 2010.

GENERAL INFORMATION

CS III INTRODUCTION

The National Cyber Exercise: Cyber Storm (CS) is the Department of Homeland Security's (DHS) capstone national-level cybersecurity exercise and represents the Nation's most extensive cybersecurity exercise effort of its kind (**Figure 1**). CS is a Homeland Security Exercise and Evaluation Program (HSEEP) Tier II exercise focusing on federal strategy and policy. The Department's National Cyber Security Division (NCSD) sponsors the biennial exercise to improve the capabilities of the cyber incident response community; encourage the advancement of public–private partnerships within the critical infrastructure sectors; and strengthen relationships between the Federal Government and partners at the state, local, and international levels. The CS exercise series provides the cyber incident response community with the opportunity to continuously learn and assess its capabilities, building on previous experience, lessons learned, and exercise findings. DHS NCSD successfully executed CS I in February 2006, CS II in March 2008, and CS III in September 2010. DHS has used the findings from these exercises to advance collective cyber incident response capabilities.

Figure 1: The Cyber Storm Exercise Series Is Part of a Continuous Process.

The CS III Exercise Planning Team worked closely with participating organizations throughout the planning and execution processes to ensure the achievement of goals and objectives. This collaboration yielded a sophisticated and realistic cyber scenario with global impact. The team planned, conducted, and evaluated CS III in accordance with HSEEP. To ensure an effective exercise, subject matter experts (SMEs) and representatives from both the public and private sectors took part in the planning, execution, and evaluation processes.

EXERCISE STAKEHOLDERS AND PARTICIPATION

CS III included participation from 8 Cabinet-level departments, 13 states, 12 international partners, and approximately 60 private-sector companies and coordination bodies. Participation focused on the information technology (IT), communications, energy (electric), chemical, and transportation critical infrastructure sectors and incorporated various levels of play from other critical infrastructure sectors. In addition, CS III included the participation of states, localities, and coordination bodies, such as Information Sharing and Analysis Centers (ISACs). International participation included public- and private-sector components from four countries (Australia, Canada, New Zealand, and the United Kingdom) and Government representatives from the International Watch and Warning Network (IWWN). During the exercise, the participant set included 1,725 CS III–specific system users, including some used by watch and operations centers that allowed for access of multiple users and shifts.

The CS III Exercise Planning Team treated all exercise participants as stakeholders (to the extent appropriate to their needs), encouraging all participants involvement in defining exercise objectives and CS Community objectives, determining success criteria for the exercise, and participating in exercise evaluation. Annex A contains a detailed list of Government entities, states/communities, coordination bodies, private-sector entities, and international entities that participated in CS III.

The Exercise Planning Team recruited CS III player organizations through a variety of means, including leveraging previous CS relationships, outreach to Government and sector coordination bodies, and building on past participation. As the third exercise in the series, CS III had increased visibility; so in many cases, prospective participants contacted the Planning Team directly to become participants. Because the exercise series is a continually evolving process, many veterans of CS I and CS II returned for CS III. These veterans engaged in further recruiting efforts, bringing on peers and partners to expand the player community and allow for the examination of additional relationships. Participation in every CS Community expanded from previous exercises. Primary critical infrastructure participation focused on chemical, energy (electric), and transportation (rail) sectors; and as previous participants, they were able to expand sector participation and integrate additional recruits. The Multi-State ISAC (MS-ISAC) assisted in recruiting states, and NCSD's International Affairs Program incorporated IWWN participation.

EXERCISE GOALS AND OBJECTIVES

Government and private sector planners and stakeholders developed CS III goals and objectives based on the current strategic and operational cybersecurity landscape, including the National Cyber Incident Response Plan (NCIRP) framework, previous exercise experience, and findings from CS I and CS II. The overarching CS III goals and objectives informed scenario development and identified focus areas for the post-exercise process and improvement efforts. CS II findings highlighted the importance of formalized interaction, information sharing and communication, and the policies that support these activities. Planners ensured CS III objectives remained particularly inclusive of these items and the broader CS II findings themes in an effort to consistently advance the exercise series.

The goals and objectives were also inclusive of community concerns and current initiatives. However, in addition to overarching CS III Exercise objectives, all CS Communities developed community-specific objectives.

Exercise goals:
- Exercise and enable the plans, capabilities, and procedures necessary to ensure the security of the Nation's broad and interdependent cyber infrastructure
- Leverage past and present efforts, initiatives, resources, and findings

Exercise objectives:
- Exercise the NCIRP
- Examine the role of DHS in a global cyber event
- Focus on information sharing issues (e.g., requirements, classified/tear-line, information condition/alert levels, thresholds, response roles and responsibilities, authorities)
- Examine coordination and decision-making procedures/mechanisms across the constituency (federal, state, private sector, international)
- Practically apply elements of past or ongoing initiatives, findings from past exercises, and other related cybersecurity efforts

PUBLIC AFFAIRS PROGRAM

The Exercise Planning Team, in close coordination with the DHS Office of Public Affairs (OPA), the Office of Cybersecurity and Communications (CS&C) External Affairs Program, and

NCSD's Outreach and Awareness Program, developed and implemented a robust Public Affairs (PA) Program to position CS III as a critical component of the Nation's efforts to promote an assured and resilient cyber infrastructure. The program incorporated input from real-world PA representatives from participating organizations who served as the PA experts for CS III.

The PA Community included federal, state, private-sector, and international entities and served as the coordinating body for this program. The Community met regularly during the CS III planning process. During these meetings, Community participants discussed real-world PA activities and media guidance.

During exercise week, DHS issued a press release publicly initiating CS III. At Exercise Control (ExCon), the kick-off event included remarks from DHS Deputy Secretary Jane Holl Lute, Deputy Undersecretary for National Protection and Programs Directorate (NPPD) Philip Reitinger, U.S. Secret Service (USSS) Director Mark Sullivan, NCSD Director Roberta Stempfley, and NCSD Cyber Exercise Program (CEP) Director Brett Lambo. During the exercise week media brief, Deputy Undersecretary Reitinger provided short formal remarks and participated in a question-and-answer session about cybersecurity, the Nation's and DHS's cyber priorities, and CS III. After the media session, CEP Director Lambo provided a tour of ExCon and answered additional questions about CS III. These activities helped build media interest and ensured national visibility for CS III.

VERY IMPORTANT PERSON VISITOR PROGRAM

DHS created and conducted the Very Important Person (VIP) Visitor Program for CS III in order to highlight the importance of stakeholder partnerships across the cyber incident response community. The program provided senior-level invitees with an overview of the CS Exercise Series and the opportunity to observe the inner workings of CS III execution. Through these activities, participants gained in-depth understanding of their organization's involvement in the exercise and the subsequent impact of their participation. The program included a CS III overview presentation and an ExCon tour. The Office of Cybersecurity and Communications (CS&C) and NCSD leadership briefed VIP Program attendees and led the tour through ExCon. Through this program, DHS continued to foster critical trust relationships with key stakeholders.

EXERCISE DESIGN SUMMARY

TRUSTED AGENT COMMUNITY

Participants voluntarily shared sensitive information across the CS III Community to support realistic scenario design and conduct useful post-exercise analysis. This information included CS III exercise specifics, Government information, and proprietary corporate data. To address security concerns and protect exercise participants, all planning and evaluation efforts were conducted within a trusted agent community. As CS III is a voluntary exercise, volunteering to participate constituted an explicit agreement to abide by the rules of the exercise. A Trusted Agent Agreement (TAA) provided the written commitment to that agreement and formalized the trust relationship. All planners and controller/evaluators (C/Es) signed and submitted a TAA to the Planning Team prior to attending planning conferences, supporting scenario design, or participating in CS Community teleconferences.

EXERCISE ASSUMPTIONS

- CS III would be conducted in a no-fault learning environment wherein policies, plans, procedures, and processes—not individuals—could be evaluated.

- Exercise simulation would be realistic and plausible and would contain sufficient detail for players to respond.
- Players would react to information and situations as presented and respond as if the simulated incident were real (e.g., reaching out to typical contacts over typical communications means).

EXERCISE PLANNING CONSTRUCT

The Planning Team divided the 18-month planning process into five distinct stages that support planning, execution, and evaluation of the CS III exercise (**Figure 2**). Within each stage, a series of events, milestones, and general planning goals moved the process forward. Throughout the process, significant cross-community interaction, public–private collaboration, and information sharing supported increased awareness of cyber-based threats, their potential implications, and the current response framework.

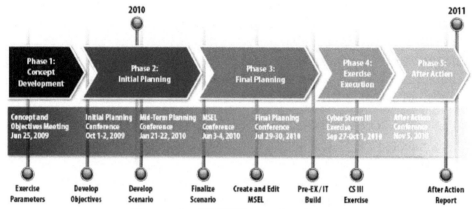

Figure 2: CS III Planning Timeline.

Concept Development Phase

During the Concept Development Phase, planning focused on establishing the exercise groundwork and building the conceptual framework for the exercise. On June 25, 2009, DHS hosted the Concept and Objectives (C&O) Meeting, the first official CS III planning meeting with stakeholders and participants. The Exercise Planning Team reviewed previous CS exercises and their outcomes and facilitated discussions on initial goals, objectives, and the participant set. Following the C&O Meeting, the Exercise Planning Team continued to recruit participants from the critical infrastructure sectors and reengaged previous participants. Other activities included defining exercise parameters and finalizing the overall planning construct based on previous experience and participant feedback.

As participants joined the planning process, the Exercise Planning Team divided the exercise planning community into more manageable and focused CS Communities. The CS Communities created forums to discuss common issues, develop objectives, and identify scenario impacts that would challenge their players. The CS III Communities included critical infrastructure (CI) sectors, energy (electric), federal, international, IT/Communications (IT/Comms), Department of Defense/Law Enforcement/Intelligence (DoD/LE/I), PA, and states.

The Exercise Planning Team implemented a "team approach" in order to develop exercise specifics such as the adversary, the core scenario conditions, and the exercise network based on previous experience. The teams included technical experts and CS veterans from across the planning community. Once developed, the core scenario conditions and the adversary created the foundation for all further planning activities. This common foundation allowed new participants to easily integrate into the established exercise storyline and focus their planning efforts on applying conditions to network and personnel specifics.

Initial Planning Phase

During the Initial Planning Phase, planners finalized exercise objectives, including the majority of CS Community objectives, and initiated scenario and adversary development activities based on these objectives and the participant set. As an objectives-driven exercise, the establishment of objectives created the foundation for all further planning activities.

On October 1–2, 2009, DHS hosted the Initial Planning Conference (IPC). During the IPC, the Exercise Planning Team reviewed the CS III exercise construct, focusing on innovations from CS I and CS II, and introduced the CS Exercise Series to new participants. The Exercise Planning Team also conducted initial CS Community breakout sessions. During these sessions, participants used a common dashboard to capture initial CS Community and organizational objectives, potential Concepts of Operations (CONOPS), likely cross-sector communication, and preliminary scenario themes. The IPC set the stage for further Initial Planning Phase activities— in particular, scenario and adversary development.

Between the IPC and the Mid-Term Planning Conference (MPC), the Scenario Team, including private sector technical experts, met on six occasions to develop the core scenario. The use of a Scenario Team and common core scenario conditions illustrated the growth across the CS series of exercises. The Scenario Team contributed to coordinated scenario development, creating a forum to vet, discuss, and achieve consensus on core scenario conditions that could be applied to participating organizations. The use of core scenario conditions as the basis for all targeted attacks ensured the exercise would represent a comprehensive National and internationally Significant Cyber Incident. In addition, using a core scenario to drive overall scenario development reflected the realities of an intentional threat and supported effective exercise management.

In developing the core scenario specifics, team members incorporated CS III goals and objectives, previous exercise findings, and previous lessons learned into scenario design. Once planners reached consensus on core scenario conditions, Scenario Team representatives provided an overview during CS Community calls and fielded questions. Throughout the planning process, Scenario Team members continued to work with CS Community planners to develop community-specific subplots. These community subplots served as different manifestations of core scenario conditions based on organization and sector specifics.

On January 21–22, 2010, DHS hosted the MPC, during which the Exercise Planning Team reviewed remaining exercise milestones, introduced exercise tools, and discussed CS III execution. Scenario Team representatives reviewed core scenario conditions during the initial plenary session to support understanding and to facilitate further discussion across the planning community. During breakout sessions, CS Communities began to develop their scenario narratives, focusing on community assets and systems to target, desired scenario conditions, and the plans that would be exercised. Community planners also identified required cross-sector and intergovernmental collaboration and potential players. Scenario Team representatives participated in these breakout sessions to support community planners and ensure narratives adhered to core scenario conditions. In addition to scenario discussions, the planning community helped to establish adversary requirements, discussed international play, and helped define exercise network requirements.

Because of the nature of the CS III participant set and their relative objectives, the Exercise Planning Team and the Adversary Team focused adversary development efforts on building the capabilities required to achieve impacts described in the scenario narratives rather than building a robust adversary network for players to track and attribute various attacks to. Adversary Team members included SMEs from the Exercise Planning Team, the intelligence community, DoD, the IT and Communications Sectors, international partners, and other cyber community experts. These planners collaborated over the course of the planning process to develop an adversary framework, update content and capabilities, and align specific attacks to logical capability groups. Members reviewed adversary characteristics, intent, and capabilities to ensure they remained realistic and in line with exercise objectives and the scenario requirements as scenario development activities advanced.

Final Planning Phase

The Final Planning Phase focused on finalizing the scenario, creating and editing the Master Scenario Events List (MSEL), and conducting all necessary pre-exercise activities. On June 3–4, 2010, DHS hosted the MSEL Conference. Over the course of two days, participants finalized their community-specific linkages, identifying expected player actions, defining projected cross-community interaction, and identifying required white cell support. Plenary sessions provided visibility into scenario linkages for all CS Communities, allowing for increased awareness of exercise play across communities and sectors. During the conference, Scenario and Adversary Team representatives worked with the CS Communities to provide technical expertise and support scenario validity.

In between the MSEL Conference and the Final Planning Conference (FPC), planners worked with their CS Community leads to develop timed exercise injects from their finalized scenario narratives. These injects would be the pieces of information distributed to players during exercise execution. In addition, planners identified individual players, organizational C/Es, and VIP candidates for the VIP Visitor Program. CS Communities continued to hold teleconferences (as needed) to monitor community progress, discuss inject development activities, and provide status updates from across the exercise planning community. CS Community leads coordinated regularly to storyboard the scenario and identify potential conflicts.

On July 29–30, 2010, DHS hosted the FPC. As the last planning conference prior to exercise execution, the FPC provided the forum to complete an exercise "dry run" with planners. Planners reviewed and vetted every exercise inject on the MSEL in time sequence. This review provided the entire community with insight into exercise flow and avoided confusing conflicts across the player set. After the FPC, planners submitted player information, finalized organizational exercise construct, trained C/Es, and refined scenario injects on the MSEL.

Concurrent with other Final Planning Phase activities, the Exercise Planning Team focused on the exercise network and ExCon setup at the USSS Headquarters. The Network Team designed and implemented a robust network to host secure exercise websites and handle phone and e-mail traffic generated by such a large-scale effort. Setup included building about 90 exercise workstations to enable the command and control and support situational awareness during exercise play.

Exercise Execution Phase

Exercise execution included participation from approximately 2,000 players, C/Es, and ExCon controllers. DHS hosted nearly 100 controllers at CS III ExCon, in downtown Washington, D.C., from September 27 to October 1, 2010. Primary ExCon functions included exercise management, flow control, inject review and development, and white cell support. ExCon controllers included full player participants representing the public sector, private industry, critical infrastructure sectors, states, and international partners. These controllers helped to manage play at their own organizations through interaction with other ExCon members and contact with their offsite C/Es. On the first day, ExCon controllers and participants out in the field conducted systems checks, reviewed read-ahead material, and prepared for live exercise play. Live exercise play ran from 08:30 a.m. on Tuesday, September 28, until 3:30 p.m. on Thursday, September 30. During this time, ExCon distributed more than 1,500 pre-scripted injects. In addition, players received hundreds of additional injects via other mechanisms, such as phone calls and classified communications.

The Exercise Planning Team implemented several activities to ensure onsite ExCon participants and offsite C/Es remained abreast of scenario development and exercise-management activities. At the beginning and end of each day, the Exercise Planning Team hosted an All ExCon/All C/E call to summarize scenario development to that point, provide a preview of projected upcoming activity, discuss any outstanding issues, and answer any questions. In addition to these calls, ExCon controllers participated in mid-day CS Community scenario updates to promote understanding across ExCon, identify potential issues, and capture cross-community play. On Friday, October 1, 2010, ExCon controllers, distributed C/Es, and local stakeholders conducted the Hotwash. During the Hotwash, the Exercise Planning Team reviewed overall exercise play and CS Community scenario results, and all participants discussed exercise outcomes and initial findings.

Post-Exercise Phase

The Exercise Planning Team implemented several different mechanisms to capture player action, observations, and post-exercise input. Each full player organization provided a C/E to monitor and control exercise play from that organization's home location. During the exercise, C/Es reported scenario developments, monitored player interaction, and discussed any issues. C/Es also participated in twice-daily All ExCon/C/E teleconferences to ensure they remained in sync with ExCon controllers and abreast of upcoming scenario activity. After live exercise play concluded, all full player organizations completed and submitted a post-exercise questionnaire. This questionnaire captured responses around key focus areas such as observed strengths and areas for improvement, plans implemented during exercise play, information sharing and collaboration efforts, the NCIRP construct, and the CS III scenario.

DHS also hosted several post-exercise events to capture further input and vet potential findings among the participant community. On October 15, 2010, DHS hosted the Quick Look Teleconference to review the Quick Look document with primary stakeholders, focusing on initial high-level findings. CS Communities also hosted teleconferences to discuss community-specific findings, capture specific observations, and identify how the community interacted within the exercise community at large. Finally, DHS hosted a final post-exercise conference on November 5, 2010, to review updated high-level findings, supporting sub-findings, and community-specific findings.

CS III SCENARIO AND ADVERSARY

SCENARIO OVERVIEW

During CS III, players responded to a series of targeted attacks resulting from compromises to the Domain Name System (DNS) and Internet chain of trust (i.e., validity of certificates and Certificate Authorities [CAs]).[3] Because of the reliance on DNS and the chain of trust for a wide range of Internet transactions and communications, the adversary challenged players' ability to operate in a trusted environment and support critical functions and trusted transactions. In addition, the adversary used these compromises to execute variety of targeted attacks against private-sector companies, selected critical infrastructure sectors, public-sector enterprises, and international counterparts. All exercise players felt effects created by the core scenario, and numerous IT/Comms, other sector, and Federal Government entities were heavily involved in resolving the situation. Overall response required significant communication and coordination per the NCIRP among a distributed and diverse player set.

The core scenario conditions allowed for the following targeted attacks to be played by a subset of CS III participants:

Scenario Targets

- **Widespread Service Update Compromise.** The adversary compromised IT and communications vendor service updates, leading to pervasive malware infections, phishing attacks, and an impending logic bomb. All exercise players experienced these conditions, and the majority of IT/Comms Community players in the public and private sectors spent live exercise play evaluating potential remediation activities and interfacing with customers and constituents. Communication of effective resolution guidance proved to be vital as typical response and recovery procedures resulted in "bricking"[4] of affected machines.

- **Energy Management System (EMS) Compromise.** Adversary compromise of EMS coding led to control systems compromises and the triggering of a logic bomb on D-Day (Monday). The logic bomb severely limited system visibility and control, leading to grid reliability issues. As the compromise persisted, major impacts on the grid, including service disruptions, occurred. Compromises to the Energy Tagging and Trading System and customer-facing websites further complicated the response. The scenario resulted in robust play from private-sector providers, EMS vendors, independent system operators (ISOs), and regulatory bodies.

- **Chemical and Transportation Scenario Linkages.** The adversary capitalized on core scenario conditions to conduct attacks against chemical and transportation companies' ordering systems and customer-facing sites. Attacks affected production and transportation of goods. The scenario resulted in play for private sector chemical and rail companies, coordination bodies, and the Government.

- **Federal Scenario Linkages.** The adversary used core scenario conditions to compromise *connect.dhs.gov* and a DHS "Chatter" account, conduct a spearphishing campaign,

---

[3] These conditions created the "core scenario" and served as a starting point for all scenario planning and customization.
[4] To "brick" infected computers, the malware would remove the IP stack, thereby preventing the computers from connecting to the network.

disrupt legitimate traffic through distributed denial of service (DDoS) attacks, compromise personal information of Government employees, and compromise customer information and financial data. Primary play occurred with DHS, Department of Transportation (DOT)/Federal Aviation Administration (FAA), Department of State, and the United States Postal Service (USPS).

- **International Scenario Linkages.** In Australia, the adversary used a series of compromises to institute sophisticated cyber command and control infrastructure extending across financial, energy, transport, water, government, and other critical sector systems. Attacks resulted in private-public coordination in Australia and some limited Usual 5 information sharing. In Canada, a massive web page defacement campaign followed by targeted malware distribution to Government IT resources and "Smart Phone" Enterprise Servers and the threat of attacks against control systems telecommunications assets prompted limited coordination, information sharing, and communications among the Usual 5. Across the IWWN nations, propagation of the Borders Worm led to massive exposure of sensitive data across political boundaries, damage to secure communications integrity, widespread outages, and bandwidth consumption.

- **DoD/LE/I Scenario Linkages.** A Defense contractor brought home a laptop (against policy) and plugged it back into the DoD information grid, leading to malware propagation. This action resulted in a compromise of the DoD military travel site, supply chain compromises of unmanned aerial vehicles (UAVs), and severe network issues at a major international company that supports the U.S. private sector and DoD (continental United States [CONUS]).

- **PA Scenario Linkages.** As attacks affecting critical infrastructure sectors intensified, a journalist contacted several companies regarding reports of cyber attacks and published a story on the National Cyber Exercise News Network (NCENN) citing specific companies and raising the public profile of attacks. In addition, various companies experienced disruption of public-facing websites, causing public imaging and communication concerns. NCENN publicized the attacks and linked events to prior investigative reports of cyber attacks and vulnerabilities, fueling public panic and widespread concern.

- **States Scenario Linkages.** The adversary targeted several states with attacks, focusing on disrupting constituent services and obtaining personally identifiable information (PII), in an attempt to create Government mistrust.

ADVERSARY OVERVIEW

To develop the CS III adversary, the Exercise Planning Team incorporated DHS Universal Adversary characteristics with real-world cyber threat elements. The simulated adversary operated as a loosely organized umbrella organization known as *FdIE* and united a diverse set of cyber capability groups to carry out large-scale and sophisticated attacks against Government, private-sector, and critical infrastructure targets. The combination of several distinct, advanced cyber attack capabilities created a uniquely qualified threat actor.

Per the exercise storyline, FdIE began as a small IT company in South America that went underground to provide illicit online services for malicious cyber activity. Individuals associated with the mock organization had cyber attack capabilities that ranged from basic "for-profit" attacks to advanced campaigns against critical infrastructure. FdIE gained experience by renting its services to clandestine individuals and groups with malicious purposes. Players were told that in the past, FdIE rented services to hacktivist groups, organized crime groups, individual actors, and even known terrorist groups. As long as the group renting the service could prove that it was not associated with law enforcement or the intelligence community and could provide the capital, FdIE would accept its business. FdIE commonly hired other groups, using their specific capabilities to complete their contracts. In the past, they hired groups for malicious software development, exploit development, and other services.

FdIE's founder was presented as a talented computer engineer with connections to the political elite and strong anti-Western sentiments. While undergoing normal recruiting operations, the founder contacted a series of capability groups with specialties in cryptography, application- and service-layer exploitation, and malicious software development, among others. The expertise of these groups, in addition to FdIE's expertise and connections to political elites, positioned FdIE to wage a potentially devastating attack on the United States and its allies.

CS III Findings

Information gathered throughout exercise planning and execution, post-exercise activities, and submission of post-exercise questionnaires revealed five significant high-level areas of findings. These findings, outlined below, incorporate perspectives of CS III participants representing the Federal Government, state and local government, coordination bodies, the private sector, and international partners. They affect the cybersecurity community at large. Sub-findings (found in the bulleted lists below) provide additional detail to the high-level findings. Observations tie high-level finding and sub-findings to specific examples and experiences from CS III.

Finding 1:

The NCIRP provides a sound framework for steady-state activities[5] and cyber incident response; however, the supporting processes, procedures, roles, and responsibilities outlined in the Plan require maturity. To truly serve as the framework for national-level cyber incident response, NCIRP concepts need to be further integrated into supporting Standard Operating Procedures (SOPs) and CONOPS, complementary response plans, and corresponding partner operating procedures.

1.1 CS III participants identified overall process concept, coordination path outlines, and incident response landscape overview as current NCIRP strengths. The NCIRP outlines a framework for coordinated response and creates a forum for decision-making.

1.2 The maturation of supporting SOPs and CONOPS will facilitate increasingly effective internal National Cybersecurity and Communications Integration Center (NCCIC) operation and external cooperation with diverse partners. As SOPs and CONOPS are vetted among the constituent community and reinforced with training, information sharing and interaction will become more streamlined and overall response will be more efficient.

1.3 As a critical component of the NCIRP, the Cyber Unified Coordination Group (UCG) roles, responsibilities, and operational tempo need to be further defined. Operational

---

[5] CS III execution primarily evaluated the transition from steady state to cyber incident response and cyber incident response actions outlined in the NCIRP. However, the ability to share the draft NCIRP with stakeholders across the public and private sectors allowed for aspects of steady-state operations to be evaluated and assessed.

details such as senior versus staff functions, teleconference schedule and agenda, and distribution of information need to be further defined and better understood across the UCG constituency. In addition, the appropriate policy and technical expertise from across the cyber community must be available to address cyber incidents.

1.4   Relationships between the NCCIC and partners will evolve based on mission expertise and capabilities as NCIRP roles and responsibilities are more clearly defined and different types of cyber incidents are addressed. In some instances, it may be more logical for NCCIC entities to prioritize information sharing and support situational awareness over developing technical solutions.

1.5   The Federal Government and the private sector should continue to define, develop, and advance information-sharing efforts and collaborative operations under the NCIRP framework. In particular, an effort should be made to identify additional opportunities for mutually beneficial interaction and determine the types of information that each side can provide, along with the most effective mechanisms and/or venues.

1.6   As the NCIRP matures further, consistent testing, training, exercising, and reevaluation of the Plan will foster greater understanding, more efficient operation, and up-to-date concepts that match the dynamic nature of cybersecurity–related issues.

1.7   With an extremely diverse player set responding to scenario play and moving toward remediation efforts, many players did not have a clear understanding of the capabilities and responsibilities of the involved parties. In particular, participants lacked a common understanding of Federal Government response authorities and where potential overlaps might exist. As Government and industry learn more about each other's roles and capabilities relational to cyber incident response, it will allow for further capabilities to be leveraged to increase overall effectiveness.

Observations

In preparation for exercise play, NCIRP Interim Version, September 2010, was distributed to CS III participants who had not been involved in the NCIRP writing community during the weeks preceding the exercise. Though many participants and players did not yet have a detailed understanding of NCIRP concepts and had yet to align their processes and procedures, the exercise created a venue for the plan to be socialized among a significant portion of the cyber response community and stressed during a simulated crisis involving a diverse player set. Players noted that once the NCIRP is released, further socialization, training, and exercising will be necessary.

During exercise play, the NCIRP provided the framework for interaction and coordination of response to the simulated cyber crisis. The NCCIC collated attack data from numerous sources, and the Cyber UCG provided a venue for high-level information sharing and decision-making—though both bodies require maturation. In particular, as players responded to exercise injects and sought to interact among the player set, they discovered that many current processes and procedures are not streamlined across the cyber response entities. In addition, the nature of relationships (i.e., informational vs. diagnostic)—particularly among NCCIC bodies and between the critical infrastructure sector coordination and NCCIC bodies and private industry—are still being defined.

Despite identifying challenges, many players recognized the strength of the NCCIC as a central mechanism for cyber incident response. In particular, federal players found that NCCIC representatives proactively engaged, passed actionable information in a timely fashion, and offered assistance when needed, allowing Federal Departments and Agencies (D/As) to implement mitigation measures. Furthermore, NCCIC collocation of cyber and communications operational capabilities (U.S. Cyber Emergency Readiness Team [US-CERT] and National Coordinating Center [NCC] Watch) enhanced the Federal Government's ability to respond to an incident affecting IT and communications infrastructures.

As stakeholders across the public and private sectors interacted to resolve scenario conditions, players expressed uncertainty regarding the current cyber response landscape. More specifically, many players noted that they did not have a clear understanding of the organizations involved, their relative roles and responsibilities, or how to interact most beneficially within the community. This included high-level coordination issues and low-level details, such as the type of information to share and the format for submission. Feedback provided to players during the exercise will help collectively communicate these processes and procedures.

Finding 2

Cyber response collaboration among private-sector companies has advanced because of targeted initiatives and understanding of mutual benefit. While public–private interaction around cyber response is continually evolving and improving, it can be complicated by the lack of timely and meaningful shared situational awareness; uncertainties regarding roles and responsibilities; and legal, customer, and/or security concerns.

2.1 An improved mutual understanding of the Federal Government's and owner and operators' roles and responsibilities in responding to Significant Cyber Incidents will facilitate public–private information sharing and create a foundation for subsequent policies and procedures. Each party possesses unique capabilities, authorities, roles, and missions to conduct cyber incident response activities. Continuing to drive toward mutual understanding will allow these entities to become increasingly complimentary and allow for a more integrated, joint response.

2.2 To effectively share information between the public sector and private industry, both parties need to have a better understanding of the type of information that could be provided to them, the value of that information, and implications for improved decision-making. Information sharing can also be supported through improved knowledge of both public and private cyber response resources.

2.3 Private-sector vendors can often serve as an "early warning system" to cyber events affecting multiple sectors because of the pervasiveness of private-sector technology products, a diverse and distributed customer base, and major support contracts across all lines of industry.

2.4 Ensuring information sharing and access to critical data among the appropriate cyber entities remains a challenge. In particular, difficulties associated with clearances, classified facility and communications access, the "tear-line" process, information sharing agreements, and sharing of proprietary data are significant issues to address. The Government should have processes in place that allow for relevant industry expertise to be leveraged during a crisis.

Observations

During exercise play, private-sector companies interacted with each other in a variety of ways to share information and work toward solutions. The chemical, electric, IT and transportation companies used coordination bodies, such as ISACs, trade associations, sector-specific agencies, and direct company-to-company contact to share information across sectors. Private-sector IT companies worked together to address compromises, alert critical partners, and develop technically viable solutions. IT players, in particular, relied on industry working groups, company relationships, and personal relationships to collaborate. Using these avenues, players worked toward solutions that could be distributed to customers and the public. However, because of security and customer concerns, Government entities had limited insight into these processes.

During exercise play, Government components aggregated available data and distributed it to constituencies through established communications means and standard formats, such as NCCIC Situation Reports (SITREPs), US-CERT products, and Federal Bureau of Investigation (FBI) reports. These activities contributed to situational awareness and supported coordination efforts across sectors. However, the data was often in raw or un-analyzed form, dealt with specific attack vectors, and did not address potential big picture impacts. In many cases, industry had little awareness of these products.

Public–private coordination during cyber response activities has evolved in recent years, as evidenced through the activities of coordinating bodies such as Sector Coordinating Councils (SCCs) and ISACs, as well as private-sector representation on the UCG. For the IT sector, the IT–ISAC served as a point of information sharing with the Federal Government—namely, with the NCCIC and US-CERT. For the transportation players, the Surface Transportation–ISAC (ST-ISAC) served as an informational conduit between the NCCIC and its private-sector members. In several cases, effective public and private interaction contributed to remediation activities. For example, in the Electric Community, coordination among private utilities and vendors, the Federal Energy Regulatory Commission (FERC), North American Electric Reliability Corporation (NERC), the Electricity Sector–ISAC (ES-ISAC), FBI field offices, US-CERT, and Industrial Control Systems–CERT (ICS-CERT) contributed to scenario resolution and the reestablishment of normal operations. The interaction among these entities illustrates the interdependent network of stakeholders inherent in the information-sharing process during a major incident. Private-sector companies also participated in UCG meetings, supporting high-level information sharing and decision-making. The exercise highlighted benefits of increased direct, two-way information sharing during a Significant Cyber Incident.

Finding 3
To foster common awareness and support decision-making during a crisis, development, distribution, and maintenance of shared situational awareness—sometimes referred to as a common operating picture (COP) or, in this case, a cyber COP—across the community is a requirement. To be most effective, this shared situational awareness should be continuously maintained during steady state and incorporate resources and inputs from all stakeholders.

3.1 From CS I to CS III, the cyber community made progress toward improved shared situational awareness during cyber incident responses. During exercise play, cross-community, interagency, and public-private-sector interaction highlighted the advancement. However, fostering shared situational awareness that is easily viewed by relevant stakeholders, accurately displays known impacts, and effectively highlights significant threats still remains a challenge.

3.2   As designated in the NCIRP, DHS "integrates and maintains [the] national common operating picture for cyberspace via the NCCIC with the direct assistance and participation" from a variety of sources and organizations. These sources span Government entities, private industry, coordination bodies, and international counterparts. Streamlining the NCCIC submission process, including the type of information and preferred format, will contribute to more effective analysis of current impacts and potential threats. It will also allow for inclusion into NCCIC products and a cyber-specific common operating picture.

3.3   Increased development and use of tools and technology at the NCCIC and across the cyber response landscape will contribute to an improved cyber common operating picture. The ability to quickly visualize current and potential impacts will foster widespread awareness and support decision-making. In addition, the ability to conduct secure communications involving all the appropriate parties will support the development, distribution, and maintenance of a cyber COP.

3.4   Inclusion of sensitive and classified information into the cyber common operating picture remains a challenge. Shared situational awareness is a critical aspect of cyber incident response; it can also play a significant role in prevention and early warning.

3.5   As the NCCIC continues to work toward operating as one unit rather than collocated individual bodies and as partner capabilities are integrated into operations, the national common operating picture for cyberspace will be improved.

3.6   During a crisis, the development of an accurate and informative common operating picture will contribute to effective decision-making by the Cyber UCG and crisis stakeholders. The ability to communicate and distribute information and solutions during crises must exist and be both understood and accepted across the cyber community.

Observations

Players dedicated a significant amount of time creating and updating a common operating picture based on scenario events, their own organization's informational needs, and inputs from partner organizations. Players worked to establish common operating pictures through activities such as requests for information (RFIs), direct contact, the development and receipt of reporting, and cross-community teleconferences. As an example, information flow between FBI and DHS Intelligence and Analysis (I&A) enhanced situational awareness regarding the adversary and led to a comprehensive cyber COP between those two agencies. Players also submitted attack information to the NCCIC to support the integration and maintenance of a national common operating picture. NCCIC players collated attack and impact information to produce SITREPs and distributed them to their constituent and partner organizations. Although these reports supported shared situational awareness, several players and C/Es noted the difficulty of visualizing the aggregate current and potential impacts of these seemingly diverse attacks. Participants found that the ability to fully understand the breadth of impacts is complicated by the fact that stakeholders have different roles, responsibilities, and systems on which they operate.

Players experienced some challenges submitting reports and attack information to the NCCIC. Although the NCCIC received input from a wide variety of sources, the information often lacked a common reporting format and a common submission method. This made the information more difficult to analyze, compile, integrate into SITREPs, and to communicate overall situational awareness. In some cases, players received SITREPs and considered them definitive and compiled from all available sources. This conclusion prevented some participants from seeking additional data from other sources. Although reports proved to be informative, players still found it difficult to quickly visualize the current and potential impacts of the simulated cyber attack.

Players also encountered challenges associated with classification, the use of common tools, and the availability of reliable communications. Exercise planners noted that although exercise play did not focus on the prevention stage specifically, players experienced classification issues concerning inclusion of sensitive preventive information, such as indications and warnings (I&W), into the cyber COP. In the case of a large-scale Internet outage, such as the one simulated in CS III, players also found they could not rely on their normal systems to communicate among the cybersecurity centers. In addition, planners discovered that cybersecurity centers do not currently have a real-time collaboration tool to support a cyber COP.

Finding 4

The National Cyber Risk Alert Level (NCRAL) is intended to inform preparedness, decision-making, information-sharing requirements, and cyber incident management activities. To increase NCRAL effectiveness, the thresholds that precipitate an alert level change, the communications and messaging that accompany a level change, and the recommended security posture and actions at each level must be further defined, widely distributed, and incorporated into organizational SOPs, Operations Plans, and CONOPS.

4.1 For the public to have awareness of changes to the NCRAL and understanding of the operational impacts, the NCRAL should have a more clearly defined distribution mechanism and be accompanied by specific messaging. The messaging should include a description of current, releasable impacts as well as recommended actions or suggested security posture.

4.2 As the NCRAL is further developed and socialized, the relationships to other threat levels, including DoD Information Operations Condition (INFOCON), the Homeland Security Advisory System (HSAS), critical infrastructure sector, and state and organizational threat levels will need to be further defined.

4.3 As the NCRAL is further developed, the following high-level issues will need to be addressed:
- Relationship with relevant authorities and related legal issues
- NCRAL and associated resource commitments
- NCRAL and associated lead authority

Observations

During exercise play, DHS raised the NCRAL on two occasions to respond to increased threat severity and widespread impacts experienced across sectors. By the end of D-Day (day one of live exercise play), the NCCIC Watch and Warning (W&W) Group recommended the NCRAL be raised from 4 (Guarded) to 3 (Elevated). The Assistant Secretary of CS&C, in consultation with the UCG, raised the NCRAL on the morning of D+1 (Wednesday). As events escalated further on the afternoon of D+1, the Assistant Secretary, again in consultation with the UCG, raised the NCRAL from 3 (Elevated) to 2 (Substantial). Following the meeting, the Assistant

Secretary notified the White House, the Secretary of Homeland Security, and Congress; the NCCIC released a notice shortly after.

Although a change in the NCRAL contributed to increased awareness of overall threat severity, individual members of the cybersecurity community and the public did not fully understand what the level change meant for them. Many players did not understand the justification for the NCRAL changes, the relative impact to their organization or sector, or the impact on overall operational stance. The NCRAL is not currently linked to alert levels established by many sectors, states, and organizations that many players are familiar with. Notification also proved to be inconsistent across the player set, particularly for players who did not have direct communication with the NCCIC or access to SITREPs. As a result, players often became aware of NCRAL changes through media articles.

Finding 5
The Government, the private sector, and the general public rely on timely, accurate, and actionable public and strategic communication to manage threats to their networks and systems. The development and delivery of effective products and public statements are critical to coordinating an effective cyber response and maintaining public confidence during an incident.

5.1   Both communication content and timing are of critical importance. Accurate messaging that incorporates the appropriate technical details, contains impact-oriented messages, and provides actionable recommendations must be balanced with the need for quick and timely communication.

5.2   The evolution of new forms of communication and social media has increased the speed with which information and misinformation spreads. Communications from official sources (i.e., the Government or affected organizations) necessitate a more proactive and rapid PA response to minimize the distribution of inaccurate information and rumors. Social media contributors are less likely to verify information before publishing it, further reinforcing the need to proactively verify the message before incorrect or inaccurate information becomes widespread.

5.3   Action-oriented messaging regarding who is in charge, who is contributing to the response, and what actions are being taken help maintain public confidence and provide a focal point for coordination of public messages.

5.4   Clear communication and messaging documents must accompany alert level changes to inform the public of the reason and the impact of the alert level change. Communication documents should focus on defining impact and establishing action-oriented recommendations or next steps. Clear and specific guidance will help response partners provide meaningful support and empower the public to protect itself, further reinforcing public confidence.

5.5   In the absence of alternative trusted information, the public will turn to traditional and social media for situational awareness. Effective and proactive engagement of traditional media and established social media sources will help manage public confidence by ensuring that information in the public domain is accurate.

Observations
In an effort to support public confidence during a cyber incident, PA players worked to stay ahead of traditional and social media reports, engage with the public, and coordinate messaging

across affected entities. Through these efforts, several issues, potential areas for improvement, and positive takeaways came to light. In some cases, players found it difficult to coordinate messaging across affected parties when consequences of the incident and expectations from media sources demanded quick public response. Differing thresholds for media engagement and differing sensitivities to acknowledgement of impacts further complicated coordination efforts. At the federal level, DHS and the Department of Justice (DOJ) coordinated public outreach at critical escalation points. The use of a joint press conference, featuring both the DHS Secretary and the U.S. Attorney General, presented a unified public image and reinforced the Federal Government's active management of the crisis.

CONCLUSION

CS III provided a realistic environment for our national cyber response apparatus to assess cyber response capabilities. DHS and participating organizations worked closely to establish the exercise's goals and design a realistic scenario that met those goals and challenged players to respond. In addition, CS III allowed the community to coordinate a national-level response to a Significant Cyber Incident as outlined in the interim NCIRP. As part of exercise play, players identified significant findings and actions at the national, state, sector, and organizational level that will need to be addressed by the cyber incident response community. Ultimately, CS III served as a critical tool that allows the cyber incident response community to examine closely the growth and evolution of cyber capabilities.

CYBER STORM III ANNEXES

General Annexes

ANNEX A.　PARTICIPANT LIST

Cyber Storm III Participants

Federal Government Entities

- **Central Intelligence Agency (CIA)**
- **Department of Commerce (DOC)**
  - National Telecommunications and Information Administration (NTIA)
  - Office of the Chief Information Officer
- **Department of Defense (DoD)**
  - Defense Cyber Crime Center (DC3)
  - Defense Contract Management Agency (DCMA)
  - Defense Intelligence Agency (DIA)
  - Defense Security Service (DSS)
  - Office of the Joint Chiefs of Staff National Security Agency (NSA)
  - Office of the Secretary of Defense, Policy
  - United States Cyber Command (USCYBERCOM)
  - United States Northern Command (USNORTHCOM)
  - United States Strategic Command (USSTRATCOM)
- **Department of Energy (DOE)**
- **Department of Health and Human Services (HHS)**
- **Department of Homeland Security (DHS)**
  - Directorate for Management
    - Office of the Chief Information Officer
  - Intelligence and Analysis (I&A)
  - National Protection and Programs Division (NPPD)
    - Office of Cybersecurity and Communications (CS&C)
      - National Cybersecurity and Communications Integration Center (NCCIC)
      - National Cyber Security Division (NCSD)
        - United States-Computer Emergency Readiness Team (US-CERT)
        - Industrial Control Systems Cyber Emergency Response Team (ICS-CERT)
      - National Communications System (NCS)
        - National Coordinating Center for Telecommunications (NCC)
    - Office of Infrastructure Protection (IP)
      - Critical Infrastructure Warning Information Network (CWIN)
      - National Infrastructure Coordination Center (NICC)
      - Sector Specific Agency Executive Management Office (DHS–IP/SSA EMO–Chemical, Dams, and Nuclear)
  - Office of Operations Coordination and Planning
    - National Operations Center (NOC)
  - Office of Public Affairs (OPA)
  - Transportation Security Administration (TSA)
  - United States Coast Guard (USCG)
  - United States Customs and Border Protection (CBP)
    - Security Operations Center (SOC)

- **DHS (Cont'd)**
  - United States Secret Service (USSS)
- **Department of Justice (DOJ)**
  - Computer Crime and Intellectual Property Sector (CCIPS)
  - Criminal Division
  - Federal Bureau of Investigation (FBI)
  - National Security Division (NSD)
- **Department of State (DoS)**
  - Computer Incident Response Team (CIRT)
- **Department of Transportation (DOT)**
  - Federal Aviation Administration (FAA)
- **Federal Energy Regulatory Commission (FERC)**
- **Internal Revenue Service (IRS)**
  - Computer Incident Response Center
- **Office of the Director of National Intelligence (ODNI)**
  - Office Intelligence Community-Incident Response Center (IC-IRC)
- **Office of Science and Technology Policy**
- **United States Postal Service (USPS)**

State Government Entities

- **California**
  - California Emergency Management Agency
  - California Highway Patrol
  - City and County of Sacramento
  - Community of Palo Alto and other Counties
  - Department of Motor Vehicles
  - Office of Information Security
  - Office of Technology Services-State Data Center
  - Office of the Chief Information Officer
  - State and Sacramento Fusion Centers
- **Delaware**
  - Delaware Information and Analysis Center-High Tech Crimes Unit
  - Department of Technology and Information-Cyber Incident Response Team
  - Delaware Emergency Management Agency
  - Cities of Dover and Wilmington
- **Illinois**
  - Central Management Services
  - Illinois Department of Human Services
  - Illinois State Police
  - Statewide Terrorism Intelligence Center (STIC)-Fusion Center
- **Iowa**

- **Iowa (Cont'd)**
  - Iowa Department of Natural Resources
  - Iowa Department of Human Services
  - Iowa Department of Administrative Services-Information Technology Enterprise
  - Iowa Utilities Board
  - Iowa Communications Network
- **Massachusetts**
  - Massachusetts Information Technology Division
- **Michigan**
  - Department of Technology Management and Budget
  - Michigan Department of Transportation
  - Michigan Intelligence Operations Center-Fusion Center
  - Michigan State Police
- **Minnesota**
  - Department of Public Safety
    - Department of Public Safety-HSEM
  - Office of Enterprise Technology
  - Minnesota Joint Analysis Center
- **New York**
  - Fusion Center
  - CSCIC
- **New York (Cont'd**
  - Office of Cyber Security & Critical Infrastructure Coordination
  - New York City-Department of Information Technology & Telecommunications
    - Chief Information Officer/Office for Technology
    - Customer Networking Solutions
    - Data Center (Network, Server Hosting)
    - Telecommunications/Network Operations Center
    - Customer Care Center
    - Security and Risk Management
- **North Carolina**
  - Agency Security Liaisons
  - Department of Justice
  - Department of Revenue
  - Department of Transportation
  - Office of the State Controller
  - Information Technology Services
- **Pennsylvania**
  - Commonwealth Technology Center
  - Department of Community and Economic Development
  - Department of Conservation and Natural Resources

- **Pennsylvania (Cont'd)**
  - Department of Health
  - Department of Labor and Industry
  - Department of Military and Veterans Affairs
  - Department of Pennsylvania State Employees Retirement System
  - Department of Public Welfare
  - Department of Transportation
  - Liquor Control Board
  - Pennsylvania State Police
  - State of Pennsylvania Chief Information Security Office
  - Securities Commission
- **Texas**
  - City of San Antonio
  - Comptroller of Public Accounts
  - Department of Assistive & Rehabilitative Services
  - Department of Information Resources
  - Department of Aging & Disability Services
  - Department of Public Safety
  - Department of Transportation
  - Governor's Division of Emergency Management
  - Health & Human Services Commission
  - Office of the Secretary of State
  - Public Utility Commission
  - Texas Commission on Environmental Quality
  - Texas Department of Criminal Justice
  - University of Texas System
  - University of Texas at San Antonio, Center for Infrastructure Assurance and Security
- **Washington**
  - Department of Information Security
  - Department of Licensing
  - Department of Labor and Industries
  - Department of Corrections
- **Washington (Cont'd)**
  - Employment Security
  - City of Seattle
- **Wisconsin**
  - Wisconsin Emergency Management (DMA)
  - Wisconsin Department of Justice/Fusion Center
  - Wisconsin Department of Military Affairs
  - Wisconsin Division of Enterprise Technology (DOA)

• **Wisconsin (Cont'd)**
– Madison Police Department
– Milwaukee Police Department
– Federal Bureau of Investigation Milwaukee Division
Industry Entities
• ABB • Air Products and Chemicals, Inc. • Areva • AT&T • Burlington Northern Santa Fe Railway Company (BNSF) • C5i • Canadian Electric Association (CEA) • Celanese • Cisco • Computer Sciences Corporation (CSC) • The Dow Chemical Company • Dow Corning • DTE Energy • eBay • Edison Electric Institute (EEI) • EMC Corporation • Entergy • Flint Hills Resources, LP • Hughes Network Systems • Intel Corporation • Internet Corporation for Assigned Names and Numbers (ICANN) • Juniper • Kansas City Power and Light (KCPL) • McAfee • Microsoft • Midwest Independent Transmission System Operator (MISO) • Neustar • Nominet • Northern Indiana Public Service Company (NIPSCO) • NTT America • Qwest • Rhodia Inc. • Sempra Energy • Siemens • Southern California Edison

- Southern Company
- Symantec
- Tennessee Valley Authority (TVA)
- Union Pacific Railroad Company
- VeriSign
- Westar Energy

Coordination Bodies

- American Chemistry Council (ACC)
- Association of American Railroads (AAR)
- Chemical Sector Coordinating Council (SCC)
- Cyber Unified Coordination Group (UCG)
- Financial Sector Information Sharing and Analysis Center (FS-ISAC)
- Information Technology Information Sharing and Analysis Center (IT-ISAC)
- Joint Telecommunications Resources Board (JTRB)
- Kansas Intelligence Fusion Center
- North American Electric Reliability Corporation (NERC)/Electric Sector Information Sharing and Analysis Center (ES-ISAC)
- Multi-State Information Sharing and Analysis Center (MS-ISAC)
- National Coordinating Center Communications Information Sharing and Analysis Center (NCC Comms-ISAC)
- National Petrochemical and Refiners Association (NPRA)
- North American Electric Reliability Corporation (NERC)
- Public Transportation/Surface Transportation Information Sharing and Analysis Center (PT/ST-ISAC)
- Rail Industry Security Committee
- SERC Reliability Corporation
- Water Information Sharing and Analysis Center (ISAC)

International Entities

- **Australia**
  - Attorney-General's Department
  - au Domain Administration Limited
  - Australian Communications and Media Authority
  - Australian Customs and Border Protection Service
  - Australian Federal Police
  - Australian Security Intelligence Organisation
  - Banking and Finance Sector
  - CERT Australia (Attorney-General's Department)
  - Communications Sector
  - Cyber Security Operations Centre (Defence Signals Directorate)
  - Defence Signals Directorate
  - Department of Broadband, Communications, and the Digital Economy
  - Department of Defence

- **Australia (Cont'd)**
  - Department of Infrastructure, Transport, Regional Development, and Local Government
  - Department of Prime Minister and Cabinet
  - Department of Resources, Energy, and Tourism
  - Energy (Electricity) Sector
  - Food and Retailing Sector
  - Transport Sector
  - Water Sector
  - Western Australian Police
  - Western Australian Public Sector Commission
- **Canada**
  - Canada Border Services Agency
  - Canada Revenue Agency
  - Canadian Security Intelligence Service
  - Communications Security Establishment
  - Department of Justice
  - Department of National Defence
  - Energy (Electricity) Sector
  - Human Resources and Skills Development Canada
  - Natural Resources Canada
  - Public Safety
    - o Canadian Cyber Incident Response Centre
    - o Government Operations Centre
  - Privy Council Office (Observer)
  - Public Works and Government Services Canada (Observer)
  - Royal Canadian Mounted Police (RCMP)
  - Transport Canada
  - Treasury Board Secretariat
- **International Watch and Warning Network (IWWN)**
- **New Zealand**
  - Centre for Critical Infrastructure Protection
  - Department of Internal Affairs/Anti-Spam Unit
  - Government Communications Security Bureau
  - Information Technology/Managed Service Providers and Security Companies
  - Ministry of Civil Defence and Emergency Management
  - New Zealand Finance Sector Security Information Exchange
  - New Zealand Control System Security Information Exchange
  - New Zealand Network Security Information Exchange
  - New Zealand Police National Cyber Crime Centre
- **United Kingdom**
  - Centre for Protection of National Infrastructure

- **United Kingdom (Cont'd)**
  - Cyber Security Operations Centre
  - Department of Business, Innovation, and Skills
  - GovCertUK
  - National Emergency Alert for Telecoms
  - Office of Cyber Security and Information Assurance
  - SCADA & Control Systems Information Exchange
  - Serious Organised Crime Agency

ANNEX B.   ACRONYM LIST

Acronym	Definition
AAR	Association of American Railroads
ACC	American Chemistry Council
ADM-EMC	Assistant Deputy Minister of the Emergency Management Committee
BIS	Department of Business Innovation and Skills
BNSF	Burlington Northern Santa Fe Railway Company
C/E	Controller/Evaluator
CA	Certificate Authority
CBP	Customs and Border Protection
CCIRC	Canadian Cyber Incident Response Center
CDC	Cleared Defense Contractor
CEA	Canadian Electric Association
CEP	Cyber Exercise Program
CI	Critical Infrastructure
CIA	Central Intelligence Agency
CIKR	Critical Infrastructure and Key Resources
CIRT	Computer Incident Response Team
CNCI	Comprehensive National Cybersecurity Initiative
CONOPs	Concept of Operations
CONUS	Continental United States
COP	Common Operating Picture
CPNI	Centre for Protection of National Infrastructure
CS	Cyber Storm
CS I	Cyber Storm I
CS II	Cyber Storm II
CS III	Cyber Storm III
CS&C	Office of Cybersecurity and Communications
CSCC	Chemical Sector Coordinating Council
CSEC	Communications Security Establishment Canada
CSMC	Cybersecurity Management Center
CWIN	Critical Infrastructure Warning Information Network
DC3	Defense Cyber Crime Center
DCMA	Defense Contract Management Agency
DDoS	Distributed Denial of Service
DHS	Department of Homeland Security
DIA	Defense Intelligence Agency
DIB	Defense Industrial Base
DNS	Domain Name System

DOC	Department of Commerce
DoD	Department of Defense
DOE	Department of Energy
DOJ	Department of Justice
DoS	Department of State
DOT	Department of Transportation
DSS	Defense Security Service
ECTF	Electronic Crimes Task Force
EEI	Edison Electric Institute
EMO	Executive Management Office
EMS	Energy Management System
ES-ISAC	Electric Sector Information Sharing and Analysis Center
EXPLAN	Exercise Plan
FAA	Federal Aviation Administration
FAQs	Frequently Asked Questions
FBI	Federal Bureau of Investigation
FERC	Federal Energy Regulatory Commission
FOUO	For Official Use Only
FPC	Final Planning Conference
FS-ISAC	Financial Sector Information Sharing and Analysis Center
FTP	File Transfer Protocol
GETS	Government Emergency Telecommunications Service
GFIRST	Government Forum of Incident Response and Security Teams
HHS	Department of Health and Human Services
HSAS	Homeland Security Advisory System
HSEEP	Homeland Security Exercise and Evaluation Program
I&A	Intelligence and Analysis
ICANN	Internet Corporation for Assigned Names and Numbers
IC-IRC	Intelligence Community-Incident Response Center
ICS-CERT	Industrial Control Systems-Cyber Emergency Response Team
IP	Infrastructure Protection
IP	Internet Protocol
IPC	Initial Planning Conference
IRS	Internal Revenue Service
ISAC	Information Sharing and Analysis Center
IT	Information Technology
IT/Comms	Information Technology/Communications
IT-ISAC	Information Technology Information Sharing and Analysis Center
IWWN	International Watch and Warning Network

JTRB	Joint Telecommunications Resources Board
LE/I	Law Enforcement/Intelligence
LTD (AU)	Australia/au Domain Registration
MC	Master Scenario Event List Conference
MISO	Midwest Independent System Operator
MPC	Mid-Term Planning Conference
MSEL	Master Scenario Event List
MS-ISAC	Multi-State Information Sharing and Analysis Center
NCCIC	National Cybersecurity and Communications Integration Center
NCENN	Cyber Exercise News Network
NCI-JTF	National Cyber Investigative Joint Task Force
NCIRP	National Cyber Incident Response Plan
NCRAL	National Cyber Risk Alert Level
NCS	National Communications System
NCSD	National Cyber Security Division
NEAT	National Emergency Alert for Telecoms
NERC	North American Electric Reliability Corporation
NICC	National Infrastructure Coordination Center
NICCL	National Incident Communications Conference Line
NIMS	National Incident Management System
NIPSCO	Northern Indiana Public Service Company
NJIC	National Joint Information Center
NOC	National Operations Center
NPPD	National Protection and Programs Directorate
NPRA	National Petrochemical and Refiners Association
NRF	National Response Framework
NSA	National Security Agency
NTIA	National Telecommunications and Information Administration
NxMSEL	National Exercise Master Scenario Event List
ODNI	Office of the Director of National Intelligence
OPA	Office of Public Affairs
PA	Public Affairs
PICCL	Private Sector Incident Communications Conference Line
PII	Personally Identifiable Information
PIO	Public Information Officer
PT/ST	Public Transportation/Surface Transportation
QA/QC	Quality Assurance and Quality Control
RCIS	Reliability Coordinator Information System
RCMP	Royal Canadian Mounted Police

RFI	Request for Information
RISC	Rail Industry Security Committee
RTA	Request for Technical Assistance
SCADA	Supervisory Control and Data Acquisition
SCC	Sector Coordinating Council
SCSIE	SCADA and Control Systems Information Exchange
SICCL	State Incident Communications Conference Line
SITREP	Situation Report
SOC	Security Operations Center
SOP	Standard Operating Procedure
SPES	SmartPhone Enterprise Servers
SSA	Sector Specific Agency
STARTEX	Start of Exercise
ST-ISAC	Surface Transportation Information Sharing and Analysis Center
TAA	Trusted Agent Agreement
TSA	Transportation Security Administration
TVA	Tennessee Valley Authority
UAV	Unmanned Aerial Vehicle
UCG	Unified Coordination Group
UK	United Kingdom
US	United States
US-CERT	United States Computer Emergency Readiness Team
USCG	United States Coast Guard
USCYBERCOM	United States Cyber Command
USNORTHCOM	United States Northern Command
USPS	United States Postal Service
USSS	United States Secret Service
USSTRATCOM	United States Strategic Command
VIP	Very Important Person